A BUS RIDE INTO HISTORY:
THE STORY OF ROSA PARKS

by Kathryn E. Lewis

illustrated by Rodney Pate

Chapters

Harcourt

Orlando   Boston   Dallas   Chicago   San Diego

Visit *The Learning Site!*

www.harcourtschool.com

Introduction

It was December 1, 1955 in Montgomery, Alabama. Riding home on the bus after a long day's work, Rosa Parks did not know she was about to become "the mother of the Civil Rights movement." Then she was told to give up her seat to a man because he was white and she was African American. Parks, who would certainly have offered her seat to an elderly person or a child, refused to move. With that one act of dignity and courage, she changed the course of American history.

Montgomery, Alabama

Growing Up

Rosa Parks was born Rosa Louise McCauley on February 4, 1913, in Tuskegee, Alabama. Her mother was a teacher. Her father was a carpenter and a builder. When she was two, Parks moved with her mother and her younger brother, Sylvester, to her maternal grandparents' farm in Pine Level, Alabama.

Rosa Parks enjoyed growing up on a farm. Her family raised chickens and cows. There was a garden with fruit, pecan, and walnut trees. For the spirited young girl and her brother, there was always something to do.

Rosa Parks loved living with her grandparents. They had an enormous influence on her life. In her autobiography, Parks wrote: "My grandfather was the one who instilled in my mother and her sisters, and in their children, that you don't put up with bad treatment from anybody. It was passed down almost in our genes."

Rosa Parks always considered her mother her first teacher. Parks's mother taught her bright young daughter how to read when she was only four. So Parks was already reading by the time she started school in Pine Level, Alabama.

At age eleven, Rosa Parks was enrolled in the Montgomery Industrial School for Girls. It was a private school founded by a woman from New England. The school's philosophy was similar to what Parks had learned at home. Every human being has enormous potential for success. Children at the school were never ridiculed or made to feel foolish.

Because she hoped to inspire children to achieve their goals, Parks decided to become a teacher just like her mother. With her own goals in mind, at grade 11, Rosa Parks headed to Alabama State Teachers' College to train to be a teacher.

Life in Montgomery

At age sixteen, Rosa Parks dropped out of school so she could help her family. Although she wanted to stay in school, Parks knew that her first responsibility was to her family. She was needed to help take care of her sick grandmother and her younger brother. She was needed to help run the family farm.

To help support her family, Parks took what she called her first "public" job. She went to work in a shirt factory in Montgomery. She would not finish school until after she was married.

In the spring of 1931, Rosa Parks met her future husband, Raymond Parks. He was working as a barber in Montgomery. As the young couple got to know each other, Parks grew to admire her future husband. She respected his intelligence, his courage, and his willingness to work for things that would improve life for his family and his race. The next year, the young couple was married.

Raymond Parks was very supportive of his wife's desire to finish high school. Rosa Parks returned to school and received her high school diploma in 1933. She was twenty years old.

In the 1940s, Rosa and Raymond Parks were active members of the National Association for the Advancement of Colored People (NAACP) in Montgomery. It was a national organization formed to combat racial discrimination in all its forms and to improve the lives of African Americans.

Over the years, Rosa Parks did many jobs for the NAACP. She served as secretary for the organization and worked with both high school students and senior citizens. She also led workshops and was involved in voter registration drives.

The Montgomery Bus Boycott

In Montgomery, a city law required African American citizens to ride in the back of the public buses. Even if there were empty seats in the front of the bus, African Americans were required to sit in the back. They could sit in the middle section only if the seats were not needed for white passengers.

On December 1, 1955, Rosa Parks got on a Montgomery city bus and sat in the middle. As the bus filled up, the bus driver told Parks to stand. When Parks refused, the bus driver called the police. Parks was arrested and taken to jail.

When news of the incident spread through Montgomery's African American community, many people were angry. A meeting was held to discuss how to protest what had happened. Community leaders proposed that African Americans stop taking the city buses. That would show the bus company how they felt. It would also cause the bus company to lose money. Finally, and just as important, it would call attention to the unfairness of the city's segregation laws.

Come to a meeting. Hear what happene

Forty thousand leaflets were printed and passed out to members of the African American community. The leaflet explained what had happened to Rosa Parks. It encouraged African Americans to avoid taking the city buses. African American ministers also helped to enlist support for the boycott.

On December 5, 1955, the bus boycott began. It was an immediate success. Ninety percent of African Americans who generally rode buses found other transportation. Many had to walk to work. Others formed carpools or used cabs driven by African Americans. As a result, many Montgomery buses were almost empty.

Martin Luther King, Jr., a young Montgomery minister, played a key role in the boycott. King was determined to bring about change. His approach was based on the idea that peaceful methods were the best way to change people's minds and hearts. He was convinced that violence would only make matters worse.

The Montgomery bus boycott was an example of nonviolent action bringing about change in society. For more than a year, the African American community of Montgomery boycotted the buses.

Meanwhile, Rosa Parks's arrest became the test case against the segregated buses. Parks was not called to testify on her own behalf. Her lawyers did not intend to defend Parks against the charges. The point was to find Parks guilty and then appeal the conviction to a higher court. So Parks was found guilty of violating the segregation laws and given a suspended sentence.

The Montgomery bus boycott lasted 382 days. It brought national attention to the issue of racial segregation. Finally, in November 1956, the United States Supreme Court ruled that all public transportation companies, such as city buses or subways, had to end segregation.

The incident on the bus led to the formation of the Montgomery Improvement Association. Dr. Martin Luther King, Jr. was elected its first president, and Rosa Parks served on its board of directors.

Because of the national interest in the bus boycott, Rosa Parks was invited to speak at various schools, churches, and organizations across the country. At first, all the attention bothered her. After a while, she came to realize that her arrest had brought many people from all over the country together to work toward justice for everyone.

Life in Detroit

Shortly after the bus boy-cott ended, Rosa and Raymond Parks moved to Detroit, Michigan. They wanted to live near her brother, Sylvester. Parks continued to travel around the country. She made appearances and gave speeches about the bus boycott and the Civil Rights movement. Her mailbox was always filled with correspondence from around the world.

In 1965 Parks began working in the Detroit office of U.S. Congressman John Conyers. She worked there until her retirement in 1988.

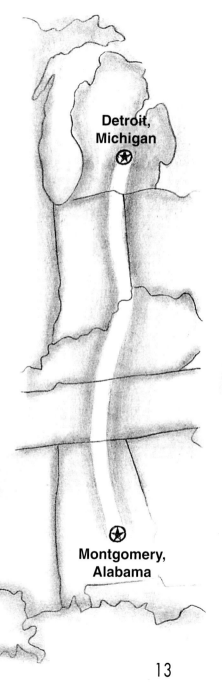

Detroit, Michigan

Montgomery, Alabama

After the death of her husband and her mother in the late 1970s, Rosa Parks began to focus her energy on starting an organization to help young people. In 1987, she worked with a partner to create the Rosa and Raymond Parks Institute for Self-Development. Parks wanted the organization to help young people continue their education and plan for the future.

Today, the Institute holds a summer program called Pathways to Freedom. Teenagers tour the country in buses. They trace the route of the Underground Railroad and learn about the history of the Civil Rights movement.

Another program at the Institute pairs young people with senior citizens. The teenagers act as mentors. They teach computer skills to senior citizens. The senior citizens counsel their young tutors about future plans. By describing their own memories, the senior citizens also give their young teachers a personal look into American history.

It has been over four decades since Rosa Parks rode into history on that Montgomery bus. The bus on which she was arrested was part of the Cleveland Avenue bus line. Today, Cleveland Avenue is called Rosa Parks Boulevard.

On December 1, 2000, 87-year-old Rosa Parks attended the opening of a library and museum built in her honor in Montgomery.

The mayor proclaimed the day Rosa Parks Day. The governor of Alabama awarded her the first Governor's Medal of Honor for Extraordinary Courage. Speaking about her strength and determination on that Montgomery bus over forty years before, the governor said, "It was an act that changed this state and our nation forever."

Rosa Parks has spent over half her life teaching love and brotherhood. In her own courageous manner, Parks has worked toward racial harmony. As she said, "Everyone living together in peace and harmony and love…that's the goal that we seek."